NATIVE AMERICAN LIFE

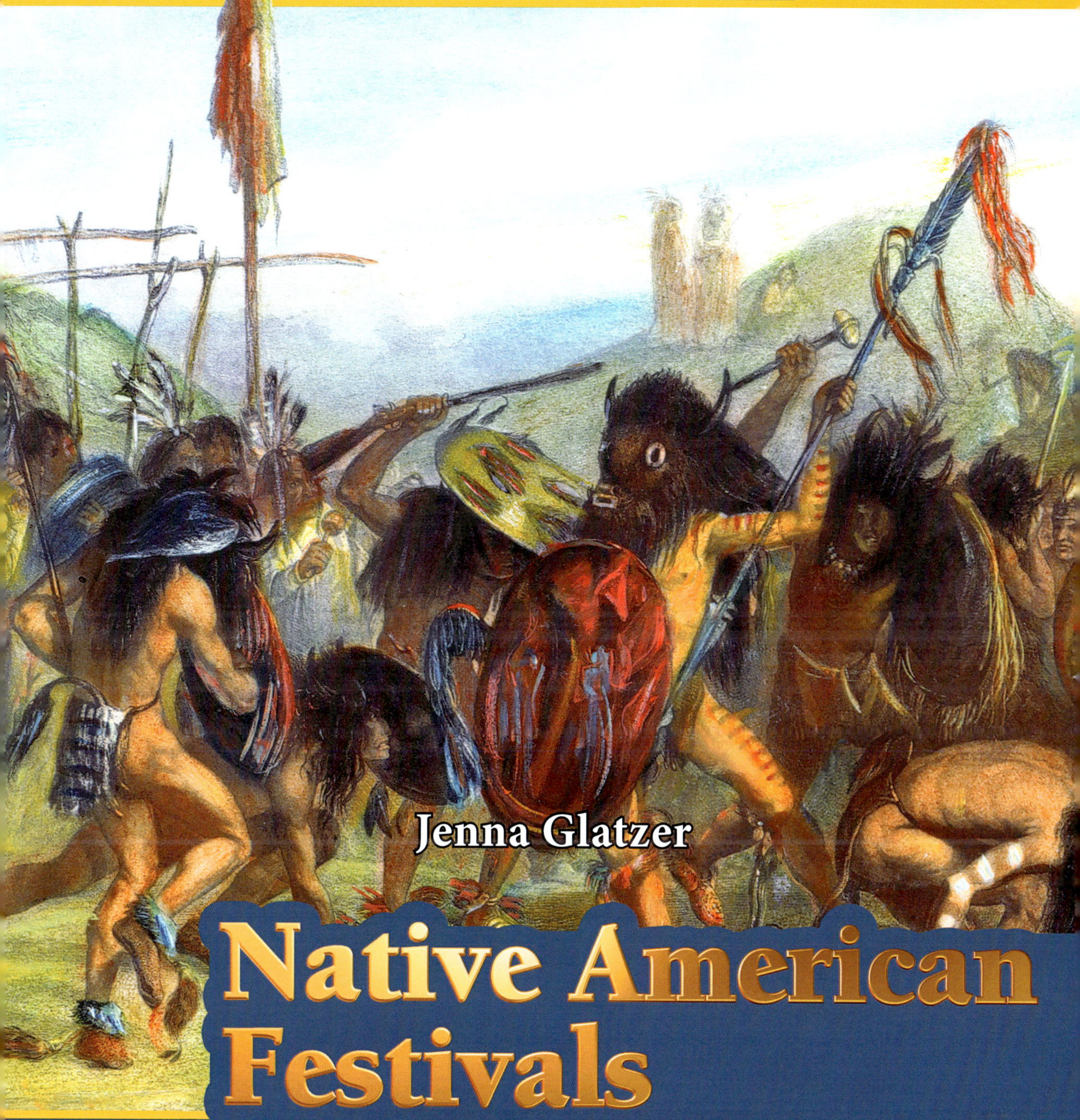

Jenna Glatzer

# Native American Festivals

LIGHTBOX
openlightbox.com

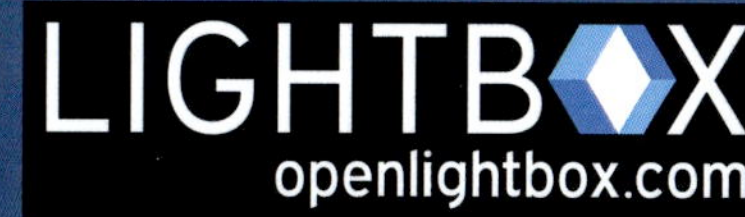

Go to **www.openlightbox.com** and enter this book's unique code.

**ACCESS CODE**

**LBXK6934**

Lightbox is an all-inclusive digital solution for the teaching and learning of curriculum topics in an original, groundbreaking way. Lightbox is based on National Curriculum Standards.

## STANDARD FEATURES OF LIGHTBOX

**AUDIO** High-quality narration using text-to-speech system

**ACTIVITIES** Printable PDFs that can be emailed and graded

**SLIDESHOWS** Pictorial overviews of key concepts

**VIDEOS** Embedded high-definition video clips

**WEBLINKS** Curated links to external, child-safe resources

**TRANSPARENCIES** Step-by-step layering of maps, diagrams, charts, and timelines

**INTERACTIVE MAPS** Interactive maps and aerial satellite imagery

**QUIZZES** Ten multiple choice questions that are automatically graded and emailed for teacher assessment

**KEY WORDS** Matching key concepts to their definitions

# CONTENTS

Dance has always been important to Native Americans. Some dances are part of a formal ceremony, some tell a story, and others are purely for enjoyment.

# Native American Festivals

Native Americans had many different kinds of festivals and ceremonies. Some of these celebrations still exist today. We can learn a lot about Native American Peoples by studying these traditions: what was important to the people and what they hoped, believed, feared, and prayed for.

Festivals and ceremonies were held for different reasons. An event took place to give thanks for good things, such as successful hunts and harvests, or to mark an important change in someone's life, such as when boys and girls began adulthood, or to communicate with the spirits, asking them to bring rain or heal sick people, for instance. A ceremony was a spiritual event, while a festival was less formal and more social. Some sacred ceremonies were only for women and some were only for men.

Different Peoples had different kinds of occasions, but they all shared things in common. For example, participants wore fancy clothing, and often sang, danced, and played instruments. They feasted on wonderful meals, held contests, smoked tobacco, and gave gifts.

Keeping traditions alive was important to the Native Americans. Thus, there were certain "rules" they followed, depending on the event. Rules about the ways to celebrate, give thanks, remember the dead, and communicate with spirits were passed down from parents to children so they would be remembered.

Many festivals and ceremonies lasted for several days. There were different traditions each day of the celebration. The activities often began before the sun rose and did not end until late at night. Even young children were expected to participate, so parents would wake them early to join in.

Most Native Americans looked forward to the festivals and ceremonies, which were usually about bringing families together, appreciating life, and having a good time. However, not all of the festivals and ceremonies were fun. Some of them involved physical torture for the warriors or scary experiences for the children. Several of the events were a test of stamina and strength. To refuse to participate in these events could cause a person to lose **status** in the eyes of the group.

## Sacred Bird

Native Americans revere eagles as sacred messengers, and have traditionally used eagle feathers in ceremonies. However, bald and golden eagles are now protected in the United States as they are endangered species. It is illegal to own, use, or sell eagle feathers, although Native Americans may keep feathers they owned before the birds were protected. The National Eagle Repository was set up in the 1970s to store eagles that are found dead. Native Americans who want eagle feathers for their regalia can apply to the repository for them.

The elaborate clothing that Native Americans wore during important events is known as **regalia**. There are different rules and traditions regarding regalia for various occasions and in different areas. For example, certain feathers, colors, beads, animal skins, or other materials are appropriate for specific dances and specific Peoples. Today, participants may spend hundreds, or even thousands, of dollars on their regalia, which is always made by hand and **unique**.

Intensive labor goes into creating ceremonial regalia. Often, items such as headdresses are gifted to a dancer or passed down through the generations.

Nowadays, there are a few festivals and ceremonies that non-natives can attend, but most ceremonies are only for Native Americans. Sometimes, Native Americans will invite a non-native friend to join in, but this is a special honor. You can't ask to participate; you must wait for an invitation.

This has happened, in part, because Native Americans are upset that some non-natives have **exploited** their customs. Sometimes, non-natives will lead their own groups teaching about "native ways." This is insulting, because many Native American ceremonies are sacred and cannot be taken out of context. For this reason, it may take time for a non-native to gain the trust needed to earn an invitation to ceremonies.

**22 Percent**
The percentage of **Native Americans** in the United States who **live on reservations**

**562**
The number of **federally recognized** Native American Peoples

**700**
The approximate number of **Nations** that took part in the **2017 Gathering of Nations**, the largest Native American gathering in North America

Shamans were messengers between the visible world and the spirit world. The rhythm of the rattles they used as they danced helped them go into a trance so they could communicate with the spirits.

# Festivals of the Northeast

Religious leaders, called **shamans**, were in charge of ceremonies, and often had special areas of power. Some might be experts in healing, for example. With the help of spirits, they would attempt to pull sicknesses out of a person's body by blowing or sucking them out and chanting. Shamans could be men or women. They were generally older people, and were highly respected.

The Iroquois, including the Cayugas, Mohawks, Oneidas, Onondagas, and Senecas, had two important ceremonies: Midwinter and the Green Corn Ceremony. Midwinter, held in January or February, lasted over a week and celebrated the new year. It was a time for thanks and forgiveness, for paying attention to dreams, and for starting new fires that would burn for the rest of the year. In Seneca Peoples, messengers known as "Big Heads" would stir ashes with a big paddle, visiting each house to announce the start of the **ritual**. Traditionally, a white dog, symbolizing purity, would be sacrificed at the beginning of the ceremony and hung from a pole covered in red paint. Later, the dog's body would be burned.

The third day of Midwinter was something like Halloween. Children, guarded by an elderly woman, walked through the village, singing and dancing in return for "treats" of tobacco. If they didn't get a present, they could take whatever they wanted. Then came the games and dances, ending with the Four Sacred Rituals, which included the Feather Dance, Thanksgiving Dance, Personal Chant, and Bowl Game.

The Iroquois were one of the Nations that celebrated the Green Corn Ceremony. It was held when the corn was ripe for harvest. It was forbidden to pick corn before the ceremony. Instead, people had to rely on leftover corn from the previous season. They would bring freshly picked corn to the ceremony to share with other families.

The Iroquois had many other festivals, mostly dedicated to nature. These included the Maple, Strawberry, Bean, Thunder, Moon, and Sun ceremonies. After the rituals, there were usually feasts. Sometimes, however, people didn't stay and eat at the ceremony. Instead, they would take the food home with them.

The Cayugas had many individual rituals to help people stay healthy and lucky. A person who died was buried in a seated position with food and tools. Ten days later, a ceremony was held. If a chief died, the **condolence** ceremony was designed to mourn the loss and to bring in a new chief.

The Wampanoag people buried their dead with their belongings, as they believed the dead person would need these things in the afterlife.

The Kickapoo People buried their dead in travel clothes with spoons, tobacco, food, and water. Funerals included feasts, singing, prayer, and silence. After someone died, people in the village left for four days, then came back and often held an adoption ceremony. (When someone died, someone else could be "adopted" to replace the dead person.)

Members of the False Face Society would search through the woods until they found a tree whose spirit "spoke" to them. They would then build a fire, offer tobacco, and cut out a section of the living tree to make their mask.

**Mourning** practices differed among Peoples. Some groups would cut their hair or blacken their faces. For the Shawnees, a replacement ceremony was common. In this ceremony, a woman could formally choose a new husband to replace a husband who had died. This happened about a year after her original husband's death.

Different Peoples had different kinds of medicine groups. Members of the False Face Society, an important part of many northeastern Peoples, wore carved wooden masks as they conducted ceremonies. Sick people could ask for help from the False Face Society, who used instruments, such as rattles and drums, as well as tobacco, in their healing rituals.

To attract good spirits, the Wyandottes of the St Lawrence River Valley held a Dance of the Fire. Participants had to touch boiling water. They also had to carry burning coals or hot stones in their mouths.

The Algonquians, who lived in Ontario and Quebec, Canada, had a Feast of the Dead. The ceremony was held each year, and included a war dance. Guests were invited to watch, and the host didn't eat while visitors were present.

## Vision Quests

Many ceremonies related to children and adolescents. For example, several Peoples had a feast to celebrate a boy's first kill during a hunt. Most also had ceremonies for male and female puberty, when boys and girls were making the transition to adulthood.

A common practice among many Native Americans was the "vision quest." Boys around the age of puberty were expected to fast, or go without food and drink, and then go on an isolated quest to find a spiritual guide to help them for the rest of their lives. They might have meaningful visions or dreams during the quest.

Members of the Fox Nation, who lived in Wisconsin, Illinois, and Iowa, thought the vision quests were extremely important for boys. Those boys who had successful quests formed a medicine pack and would perform in two ceremonies every year.

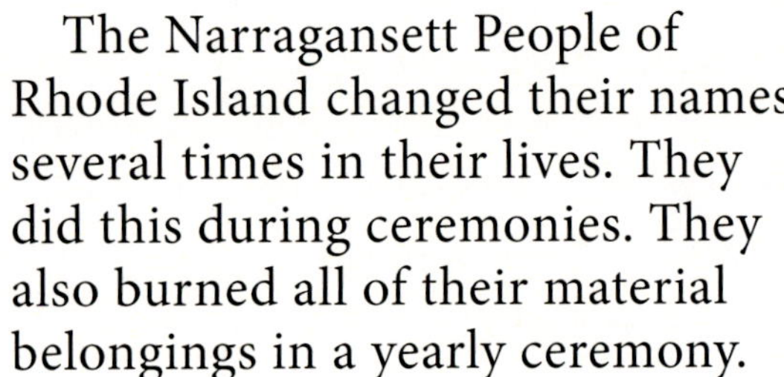

The Narragansett People of Rhode Island changed their names several times in their lives. They did this during ceremonies. They also burned all of their material belongings in a yearly ceremony.

For the Anishinabe People, dreams were important. In order to become a member of the Grand Medicine Society, or Midewiwin, a person had to report that he or she was having specific kinds of dreams or visions. The person then followed instructions, waiting to find out if he or she would be accepted.

New members of the society, who were known as Mides, were chosen during a secret yearly meeting, and injected with a sacred shell to gain spiritual powers. After this, they wore medicine bags around their necks. Mides were considered to be both spiritual leaders and healers.

The Midewiwin Dance probably arose in the 1600s because of the high death rates due to disease. Native Americans believed that sickness and disease came from the **supernatural**. Therefore, they turned to the spirits to cure them.

Bears were significant in many festivals and ceremonies. The Lenape People who were part of the Algonquian Nation, had food-related ceremonies like the Iroquois, but their most important yearly festival was the bear sacrifice each winter. Bears were **revered** by the Anishinabe People, too, and they also had a Sacred Bear Ceremony. The Micmacs of Quebec and the Maritime provinces believed that bears could change themselves into other kinds of creatures.

Mides and other healers often wore special clothing, such as a healing shirt.

The Delawares had a Big House Ceremony every fall. It lasted about a week, and included storytelling, singing, dancing, and feasting. During the 19th century, they also held a Grease Drinking Ceremony. Participants would drink the grease of a bear or hog and pour some of it into a fire in the hope that great visions would come to them.

The Shawnees had a Spring Bread Dance to ask for a good harvest, and a Fall Bread Dance to express their gratitude for the harvest and ask for a good hunting season. They also had a War Dance in August. For as long as they lived, unless they misbehaved, the same 12 men hunted for these ceremonies and the same 12 women cooked the feasts.

**4**
The number of **days and nights** a person on a **vision quest** might **fast**

**10 Years**
The **frequency** with which the **Wyandottes** held a **Feast of the Dead**, when they honored their dead and **wrapped their bones for burial** in a common grave

**20 Years**
The amount of time men and women might **study** to **reach the top level** as a **Midewiwin** healer

The Green Corn Ceremony was a time for Seminoles from different areas to get together, for disputes to be settled, and for medicine bundles to be renewed.

# Festivals of the Southeast

The Black Drink Ceremony was held by the Choctaws, Creeks, and Cherokees, who made a drink full of caffeine and served it in a **conch** shell or pottery bowl. In normal quantities, this could act like coffee, giving an extra boost of energy. However, in large quantities it would make people vomit and sweat heavily. This was supposed to cleanse their bodies and minds to make them pure. Alabamas began almost all of their ceremonies and councils with a "black drink" tea.

During the Green Corn Ceremony, also known as *itse selu*, or Busk, all of the Native Americans in this region did some cleaning, making sure their houses and common areas were neat and clean. The ceremony included purification rituals, meant to cleanse the body and the mind. All household fires were put out, and a high priest would light a new main fire. People would use the main fire to light new fires for their homes. Some Peoples held the ceremony for the forgiveness of crimes.

The Cherokees held the Green Corn Ceremony when the last corn crop had ripened. It lasted for four days. After the sundown dances had finished, storytelling would begin. This was a favorite part of the ceremony for children.

The Seminole Stomp Dance is a traditional part of the Green Corn Ceremony. It is performed several times in an evening during the first few days of the ceremony, and everyone is encouraged to take part.

Seminoles still take part in the Green Corn Ceremony, meeting in the Florida Everglades. An important part of the ritual for the Seminoles is the medicine bundle. Seminoles believe that this bundle holds magic powers, and they fear that their Nation will die if anything bad happens to it. Therefore, it is hidden in a secret spot in the swamp, and only the medicine man is allowed to touch it. Several times throughout the Green Corn Ceremony, the medicine man opens the bundle to make sure all of the contents are safely in place. Inside are stones, powder, bones, snake fangs, and other items. Men and women perform several dances around the bundle, honoring different animals. Then, the medicine man goes back into the swamps to hide the bundle until the following year.

**Lacrosse** and other sports and games were important to Native Americans in the southeast. For some, sports included ceremonies and rituals involving gambling and tobacco. Days before a lacrosse game, Choctaws would conduct ceremonies. Shamans would help the players by boosting their spiritual power to help them win. Both the sport and the gambling beforehand were dangerous businesses. The gambling might damage a person financially, and the lacrosse might leave a person with broken bones. There weren't many rules, and the game was often played to settle arguments.

Stickball is a forerunner of lacrosse. In the past, the Choctaws played it as a way of settling disputes. It was called "Little brother of war."

In Chickasaw ceremonies, two head priests, known as hopaye, led the rituals. They wore special clothes and interpreted spiritual matters. Chickasaws danced for fun and for spiritual purposes. Today, they have an annual festival each fall, with traditional foods such as cracked corn, pork, and poke greens.

Village men painted their faces during ceremonies. When someone died, his or her face would be painted, too. The Chickasaws had elaborate ceremonies for the dead, burying them in sitting positions in graves under homes. For three days after someone died, there were no social activities in the village. To Chickasaws, it was not acceptable for anyone to refer to dead people directly by name, as it was felt that this would draw the dead person's ghost to whoever said the name.

Tobacco was an important part of almost all public ceremonies in the southeast. Medicine societies used tobacco juices to cure sickness and ease insect bites. Tribal councils smoked tobacco before discussing war matters. Creeks scattered it around new houses to keep ghosts away. Native Americans saw tobacco as a spiritual tool. The smoke was a prayer that was going up to the Great Spirit. They smoked it to keep peace, change the weather, cure illness, and more. When European settlers arrived, they began selling tobacco for profit, which the Native Americans considered to be a great insult.

In the Natchez Nation, nobles had to marry commoners, called "stinkards." When the noble died, his or her spouse would be sacrificed, as would any servants. They were supposed to provide the deceased with company in the afterlife. The noble would be laid out on a platform, and his house would be burned. Commoners would usually be buried in the ground.

Some Native American groups have made cloth paintings that show tobacco smoking at Sun Dance ceremonies.

The bodies of chiefs would be removed later, so their bones could be cleaned, wrapped in deerskins, and buried next to the bones of past chiefs. It was believed that if a person behaved well on earth, he or she would be rewarded in the afterlife. If a person behaved badly, he or she would wind up in the grave.

When a Choctaw died, his or her head was painted red. Sometimes, an animal might be sacrificed to travel with the person to the land of the dead. At certain times throughout the day, there were "official" times for mourning and crying. The Choctaws paid people to mourn for them. The dead person's house was burned down, and the body was left out to **decompose**. Later, someone would scrape off any leftover flesh and return the bones to the person's family.

The Chitimachas had a six-day Midsummer Ceremony, held in a small temple. Young men were initiated as adults during this ceremony, and were expected to fast and dance until they wore themselves out. The Chitimachas also had interesting customs surrounding death. It is thought that they had "Buzzard Men" who would take a dead body, take off all the flesh, and give the clean bones back to the deceased person's family for burial. The people also held ceremonies when a war chief 's bones were buried.

A number of Native American Nations, including the Choctaws and the Natchez, let their dead decompose on a raised platform.

When Shakalo dancers entered or exited a Zuñi village, the people would toss cornmeal on them as a sign of respect.

# Festivals of the West and Southwest

In desert areas, rain is rare, but it is important for crops, livestock, and people. The Zuñis of New Mexico had many chants and dances to ask the spirits to bring rain. Shakalo is the Zuñi name for these messengers for rain.

The Zuñis had a Shakalo Festival every winter. They prepared for it all year long, and the six men who were chosen as spirit dancers went off to hidden areas to practice their chants and dances. The Shakalo dancers wore huge masks with feathers and working beaks. They didn't wear the masks on their faces. Instead, they held their masks on tall poles, and the giant skirts of the masks covered their whole bodies.

People would touch up their homes, or even build new ones, in preparation for the festival. It was an honor to have one of the Shakalo dancers visit your home. The dancers would dance all night, and were careful to perform the dance steps perfectly. They were afraid that, if they did not, it would bring their people bad luck.

Navajos created sand paintings for the Blessing Way Ceremony. The images were taken from traditional Navajo stories. After the ceremony, the paintings were destroyed.

The Navajos had two main ceremonies, but they were quite different from one another. The Blessing Way Ceremony was used to bring good luck and protection. The leader of a Blessing Way Ceremony needed a special bundle of stones and soil from sacred mountains to perform the ritual. The Enemy Way Ceremony was held to protect warriors from the ghosts of men they had killed. Singers and leaders held parts of the ceremony in different places over several days.

The Hupas of California built large houses just for ceremonies. They held a Brush Ceremony for healing that is still practiced today. Each fall, they had an Acorn Ceremony. Women weren't allowed to participate, except to grind the acorns for the ceremony.

The Wiyots held a Brush Ceremony when a child was sick and a Victory Dance when an enemy was killed. The women were allowed to dance in the Victory Dances, which was unusual. Most Native American Peoples would not let women join in this kind of dance. The Wiyots also had an unusual version of the World Renewal Festival, which several Peoples celebrated. The festival included dances, **recitations**, displays of tools, and decorations. For most Peoples, this was a complicated affair, but the Wiyots kept it simple and did not hold it often.

The Miwoks had two kinds of ceremonies, sacred and profane. Sacred dances were formal. The dancers wore fancy clothing and worried that spirits would harm them if they did not handle ceremonial items correctly. Profane, or non-sacred, dances were meant for fun, and could not bring harm to those involved.

Although most Native Americans placed great importance on vision quests during male puberty, for many Peoples of the West and Southwest, the ceremonies surrounding female puberty were more important. A girl was often separated from the rest of the group. This was the time for her to learn how to become a good wife.

Pomo girls stayed in a special hut, and were given specific instructions. Costanoan girls stayed in their homes, and their diet was limited. The Cahto ceremony lasted for six days, and the girls were expected to behave calmly and quietly for the next five months.

Achumawi girls were not expected to hide away. Instead, they had a 10-day feast with their group. The following month, they had a celebration for nine days. Each month after, they would have a celebration, each lasting one day less than the last. On the tenth month, the ritual was over. The girl was officially considered a woman. In these California Peoples, a girl usually got married soon after, or even before, puberty, and her parents often chose her husband.

## Rite of Passage

In Serrano ceremonies for male puberty, boys would be given a special drink made from jimsonweed to give them "visions." They would then dance around a fire and learn songs. Afterward, there was a feast and gift giving. In many groups, the boys' noses would be pierced, and they were expected to go on vision quests.

The Apache ceremony for female puberty was known as the Sunrise Ceremony, or na'ii'ees, and lasted four days. Girls would be covered in a mix of cornmeal and clay. They would dance and run in all four directions, and be filled with the spiritual energy of White Painted Woman. According to Apache legend, White Painted Woman was the first woman. She survived the Great Flood by floating in a shell, and her two sons saved the Apaches from their enemy, Owl Man Giant. When she was an old woman, White Painted Woman met her younger self and merged with her so she could become young again.

This ceremony is still held today, but only about one-third of Apache girls celebrate, and ceremonies don't always last for four days anymore. Part of the reason is that it is so expensive. The total cost averages about $10,000. Several people must be paid, including the medicine man, the sponsoring godmother, and the dancers. The family must also pay for food for the whole community and the elaborate regalia.

## Bulletproof Shirts

The Ghost Dance was first performed in the Great Basin area in 1889. The ritual soon spread throughout the Native American Peoples of the West. The people believed that performing the dance would cause the buffalo to return. It would also raise the spirits of dead Native American warriors, who would help force Europeans to leave a Nation's lands.

Some of the dancers wore special, colorful shirts, called ghost shirts. They believed that these shirts would keep them safe from harm and protect them against bullets. However, a tragedy proved this belief to be false. In December 1890, the U.S. cavalry attacked a group of 350 Sioux who were camped at Wounded Knee Creek, and massacred hundreds of unarmed men, women, and children.

During the Hopi Snake Dance, which is held in August, the dancers hold live snakes in their mouths. They wear red garments with a black zigzag pattern that represent the snake.

The Hopis of Arizona had some of the most varied and complex ceremonies of all Native American Peoples. Some of their ceremonies were masked and some weren't, and all of the important ceremonies lasted for nine days. They had ceremonies for rain, to honor corn, to remember their legends, to celebrate harvests, and more. Males belonged to one or more ritual societies: warrior, rain, hunt, and medicine. The rain chief held an important role. It was his job to attract the Horned Water Serpent. The snake was the focus of a special rain dance known as the Snake Dance. It was believed that the snake represented the link between the sky and Earth, so they would ask the snake to get the sky to shower down on Earth.

The Powamu Festival was important for Hopi children. During the festival, children around age eight were initiated into kachina societies. Kachinas were spirits who lived in the world below for half of the year, then inhabited the bodies of Hopis for the other half. Kachinas might be male or female spirits, but they could also be animal spirits. Men wearing masks assumed the persona and power of the kachinas. They would give gifts to children when they were good or punish them when they misbehaved. They also conversed with the gods on behalf of the villagers.

At the festival, the kachina chief would invite the children into the **kiva**, sing a song about the underworld, and bless them by sprinkling them with water and touching them with ears of corn. Then, three evil-looking kachinas would come in, howling and carrying whips. They whipped the children lightly four times each, then whipped each other. The chief gave the children presents, and they went home to feast. The next day, the children prayed and were given new names. Finally, the kachinas took off their masks and danced for the children, showing them that they were ordinary men. The children were sworn never to tell anyone the secret identities of the kachinas. The boys might grow up to become kachina dancers themselves one day.

Like other Nations, the Peoples of the Great Basin region thought bears represented special power. They had a late-winter Bear Dance to honor these animals. These Peoples did not have many ceremonies, though, because they were more occupied with survival than celebration. However, they did have Round Dances once or twice a year. During a Round Dance, people held hands and circled a tree or pole, giving thanks for antelope hunts, rabbit hunts, and harvests. Some of them also held a Round Dance to encourage salmon to come out and then another one to give thanks for their arrival.

Hopi children were given carved and painted wooden kachina dolls. The dolls were not to play with. They were to teach the children about spirituality.

The Southern Paiutes had an important funeral ritual. After someone died, mourners were not allowed to bathe until the annual Mourning Cry Ceremony. They washed themselves during this ceremony, thus ending the official period of mourning.

The Apaches avoided bringing up the subject of death. They were so afraid of ghosts that they avoided funeral ceremonies as much as possible. The Apaches had a great respect for elderly people. However, once somebody died, they wanted to get rid of the body as soon as possible. Sometimes, the face of a deceased person would be painted, but then the body would be buried quickly. The Apaches would even ask non-Apaches to bury their dead for them.

Traditionally, Apache children were kept from seeing a dead person. They also did not mix with any children who had had a family member die recently in case they were affected by ghosts who resented the living.

**2 Weeks**
The time it takes to **prepare** for the **Snake Dance**

**500**
The approximate number of **Hopi kachina spirits** who were a mix of male, female, and animal spirits

**1000**
The number of **traditional designs** the Navajo **use** in the **sand paintings** they make as part of their curing ceremonies

# Native American Festivals

Festivals and other ceremonies were important to Native Americans, whose spiritual beliefs were part of their everyday life. Many of the ceremonies related to the struggle to survive, such as asking for help before a buffalo hunt or giving thanks for the corn harvest, or to transitions in life, such as puberty or death, or to communication with the spirit world.

**Nulukataq**
Barrow, Alaska

Barrow, Alaska, holds the largest of the Nalukataq spring festivals, which are usually held in June.

**Celebration**
Juneau, Alaska

*Celebration* is held in Juneau, every second June. Over 5,000 people attend the festival of the Tlingit, Haida, and Tsimshian cultures.

**Potlatch**
Alert Bay, Canada

The U'mista Cultural Center houses potlatch artifacts that were returned to the Kwakwaka'wakw by the Canadian government.

**Crow Fair**
Crow Agency, Montana

The Crow Fair is the largest modern Native American encampment, with about 1,500 tepees set up for the four-day celebration.

**National Eagle Repository**
Commerce City, Colorado

Native Americans can apply to the National Eagle Repository in Colorado for eagle feathers to use in ceremonies.

**Gathering of Nations**
Albuquerque, New Mexico

The Gathering of Nations, held in Albuquerque, New Mexico, every April, is the largest powwow in North America.

Powwows are not only a celebration of Native American culture, they are also a means of passing cultural traditions down the generations.

# Festivals of the Great Plains

The Poncas started what we now call **powwows**. They called this gathering the hethuska. It began as a formal ceremony for the Poncas to celebrate good fortune and happiness, such as when a baby was born or when crops were bountiful. They shared the ritual of the dance with other Peoples, and, in the 1920s, some Peoples held powwows that other Nations could attend. The event became known as the Grass Dance, and it was different from the traditional sacred Native American dances. This dance wasn't religious or spiritual. It was just dancing for the sake of dancing.

The term *powwow* comes from the Narragansett word "taupowaw," which means "a wise speaker." Powwows originally referred to people with special abilities; they performed in healing ceremonies, they interpreted dreams, and they helped ensure success in battles. Over time, the name was applied to Native American festivals.

Today, powwows are open to Native Americans and non-native visitors alike. They are colorful celebrations of Native American traditions and family that are held all over the country throughout the year. They last for one weekend each, and usually include competitive dancing, singing, craft shows, storytelling, and great opportunities for Native Americans to mingle.

The material used to make a pipe varied, depending on what was available. Plains Native Americans often used a reddish material known as pipestone.

Many rituals had a more serious function than powwows, however. The Plains Peoples, who were primarily hunters, had an important ceremony to ward off battles. Horseback Nations followed the buffalo from place to place, and often found themselves running into competing Peoples. To keep peace between groups, all the Plains Peoples respected the ritual of sharing tobacco from a carved stone bowl. It was a sign that they would respect a neutral ground and not fight with each other. Men often wore a beaded pipe bag as part of their regalia.

By the 1750s, almost every Plains People also celebrated a four-day festival commonly known as the Sun Dance. However, different groups called it by different names. For example, the Poncas called it the Mystery Dance, and the Cheyennes called it the New Life Lodge. If someone had a dream about holding Sun Dance, then he would be the leader of it.

The Plains Peoples built a Sun Dance medicine lodge, which looked like the skeleton of a tent. The lodge had no solid walls or material over the structure. Instead, there was a wooden pole, the sun pole, in the middle, with a buffalo head hanging from it. Poles were connected to it to create the shape of the lodge. Branches and leaves were piled up around the structure to fill in the gaps. Sacred ceremonies were held inside.

The Sun Dance was the most important religious ceremony for many Native American Nations.

## Dance with a Difference

The Blackfoot People of Montana, and of Alberta in Canada, had a Sun Dance similar to that of other Plains Peoples, but with one important difference: a woman led the ceremony. For the first four days, the camp moved each day. On the fifth day, a medicine lodge was built. On the sixth day, they danced, blew whistles, and practiced self-torture. For the last four days, the men's societies would perform rituals.

Piercing was an important part of the Sun Dance. It was seen as a sacrifice to ensure the well-being of the Nation.

The Sun Dance was meant to help communities and individuals gain supernatural power. There was dancing, singing, and drumming. Even though the drummers and singers were allowed to take breaks, the dancers could not, and they often passed out from heat exhaustion or **dehydration**. They were expected to keep going, so they did, dancing back and forth through the lodge. They were also supposed to look straight at the sun while they danced.

During the festival, young warriors would fast, dance, and pray. They were allowed to sleep for only about an hour each day. Then, wooden skewers were pushed through the skin on their backs or chests, and they were attached to the sun pole by strips of rawhide. While others performed the Sun Dance, the warriors on the pole would tear their skin until they yanked themselves free from the pole, proving their power and representing the way a warrior might break free from capture by an enemy. This kind of sacrifice was supposed to help the participants have spiritual visions and dreams. Today, most of the torturous elements of ceremonies like this have been removed.

The Pawnees had a similarly brutal ceremony. In the Captive Girl Sacrifice—also known as the Morning Star Sacrifice—Pawnee warriors would kidnap a girl from an enemy People. They would take her to their village and treat her well for four days. Then, they would put her in a special robe, and paint her body half black and half red.

They would then tie her to a wooden frame, and shoot her in the heart with arrows. Her blood would drip onto buffalo meat, which the people would then eat. A warrior would paint his face with her blood. The Pawnees believed that this would ensure they had good crops and special power from the forces of nature.

In 1816, a man named Petalesharo cut the girl free just before she would have been killed. Many people thought that Petalesharo should have been killed for letting her go, trading his life for hers.

The practice of the Captive Girl Ceremony came to an end soon after Petalesharo saved the girl from death. Petalesharo later became the chief of his People.

The buffalo provided almost all of the needs of Plains Nations. A Buffalo Dance often preceded the Sun Dance. There were ceremonies to call the buffalo, and a ceremony of thanksgiving after a successful hunt.

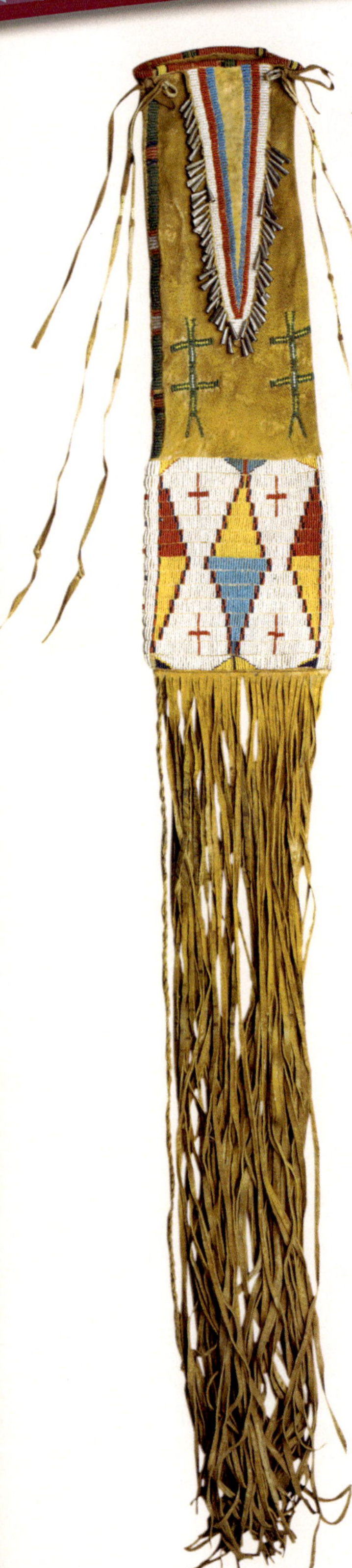

Cheyenne women had a **quilling** society, with its own ceremonies. There were different levels of membership, based on what kinds of items a member had learned to craft. A beginner might only know how to make moccasins, while a more advanced member could make buffalo robes, back rests, and other items. When a member was promoted to a new level, she invited all the members of that level to a feast to celebrate her first new project. Each woman would share stories about the items they had quilled, and then a tribal member would come to witness the woman quilling her project. That witness would receive a gift. Then, members would offer prayers and eat.

Women were not allowed to participate in the Cheyenne Sacred Arrow Ceremony. Cheyennes believed that spirits had given their ancestors four sacred arrows on a mountain. The Cheyennes had an arrow keeper, and he was the only person allowed to go into the lodge where the sacred arrows were kept in a bundle wrapped in animal hide. This keeper held his position for life.

Cheyenne women used porcupine quills and sometimes bird feathers for quilling work. The quills were dyed with plant dyes.

When the Cheyennes traveled, the arrow keeper held onto the arrows, and guards watched over him. The Sacred Arrow Ceremony was not held often. It was a secret ceremony designed to remove evil, such as, for example, when a Cheyenne killed another Cheyenne. The ceremony was conducted for four days, and the village was quiet while fires burned. Only the males who were involved with the ritual were allowed to see or touch the arrows. Cheyennes believed that, if a woman looked at the arrows, she would die.

Four was a sacred number for many Plains Peoples, and ceremonies often lasted for four days. Before a battle, Dakota warriors usually took part in a four-day ceremony that included a war dance.

Singing, feasting, speechmaking, and dancing are traditional parts of Northwest culture. *Celebration*, held in Alaska every second year, is an opportunity for the people of the Northwest to rejoice in their heritage.

# Festivals of the North

A Winter Spirit Dance was intended to help people stay in good spirits throughout the long, cold winter months of the north. A narrator would tell stories about the People's history or stories with lessons about improving lives. Sometimes, a story would be told over several nights.

The Kwakwakw'wakws of Vancouver Island, Canada, held a winter ceremony each year. Winter was the most sacred season, and the ceremony was announced by giving out red cedar bark ornaments. Members of the Grizzly Bear Society would wear grizzly bear claws on their hands, or cover themselves with a bearskin.

Grizzly Bear Dancers and the Fool Dancer, or nutamat, made sure everyone behaved at the ceremony. A Grizzly Bear Dancer would intimidate people with his power, and the Fool Dancer could attack people with sticks, stones, or even axes if they didn't behave properly. The Fool Dancer often acted "crazy." When the dancers moved one way, the Fool Dancer would move the opposite way. It was thought that the spirits who gave power to the Fool Dancer had long, runny noses, so whenever anyone mentioned anything about noses or smells, the Fool Dancer would throw a tantrum.

The Hamatsa initiate wore pieces of hemlock plant to represent his wild state.

The Hamatsa Ceremony was an important dance ritual. Each year, the Hamatsa Secret Society would select a young man as an **initiate**. He would live in the woods for a few months and learn the traditions of the society. At the Hamatsa Ceremony, people would perform dances to call forth the spirit of a cannibal giant. The young man would then return and bite people. According to legend, he would also eat skin from mummified bodies of slaves. At the end of the ceremony, the initiate would return to normal,"healed" by the power of the ceremony.

Participants in the ceremony would often get new names, according to their job for the ceremony. In fact, Kwakwakw'wakws changed names repeatedly. If a chief died, his replacement would be given his name. Names were often given as gifts. For example, when a man got married, the wife's father would give the groom a new name.

**Bowls** In the 1800s, carved bowls, often made from cedar, were given as potlatch gifts.

All around the Northwest, a **potlatch** often followed ceremonies. A host would give a potlatch to show a change in his status or to erase shame. The potlatch usually consisted of speeches and a feast or feasts. It always included gift giving. Guests would receive piles of gifts—pieces of the host's property. If they accepted them, the host would know they had accepted his change in status or accepted his "payment" for an embarrassment. These potlatches were often so extravagant that a chief would be left poor afterward.

**Eulachon** These small fish were treasured for their oil. A dried eulachon could be used as a candle. Eulachon or eulachon oil was one of the most valued gifts.

Memorial potlatches lasted for several days, and had two main purposes: to honor the dead and to help repair homes in the village. The chief's wife would ask relatives for donations of belongings and time, and, during the ceremony, the relatives would repair homes in the village, including the chief's. At the end, the chief would give gifts to those who helped—although the gifts usually included items they had given as donations at the start of the ceremony.

### Potlatch Gifts

Potlatches were often a way of proving one's wealth. Rival chiefs would invite each other to potlatches as a challenge. At the end, they would know who was the wealthier chief because the other would be left with nothing. All the people who attended a potlatch were given a gift appropriate to their rank. To many Kwakwakw'wakw, songs were the most precious item of all. People would pass a song down through their family. To be given a song was a great honor.

**Copper** To the Kwakwakw'wakw Nation, copper was one of the greatest signs of wealth. The copper was beaten into a shield shape. Only chiefs were allowed to own copper. Each piece of copper had its own name.

**Chilkat** A chilkat was a blanket made from goat hair and shredded cedar bark. Each blanket could take a year to make. Chilkats were treasured gifts.

**Ladles** Wooden ladles were used in the feast and then given away as gifts to guests.

Blanket tossing is a feature of the Iñupiat Nation's three-day spring whaling festival called Nalukataq, meaning "to toss it up."

The Peoples of northern Alaska had special ceremonies when the first whale was captured each season. Whale hunting was dangerous, so every time a boat crew came back from a successful trip, it was cause for celebration. One custom involved the men using a walrus hide as a human-powered trampoline. One man would stand in the middle of the hide. The others would lift the hide to throw the man up into the air. He would try to land on his feet, but that could be difficult. This blanket-tossing game is still practiced today.

The Peoples of the Plateau region had many interesting ceremonies. During the Blanket Ceremony, people would gather in a **tepee**, with a blanket blocking the entrance. The room would be dark and smoky. People offered tobacco, and sang to the spirits to invite them in. Leaders used this ceremony to ask questions of the spirits and to ask for help. The people also had Weather, or Chinook, Dances, to ask the spirits to bring rain or melt the snow.

**50 Feet**
**(15 meters)**
The **height of some totem poles** carved by **Northwest Native Americans**, often as part of a potlatch

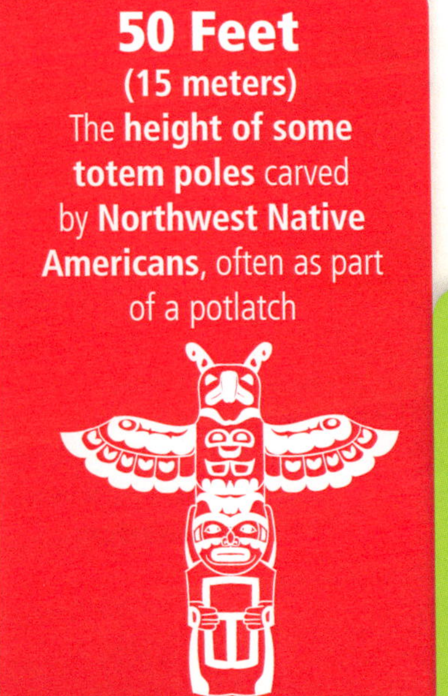

**2–4**
The number of **whales needed** to feed an **Alaska Native Nation for a year**

**1 Year**
The time it can take to **prepare for a potlatch**

Blue Jay Dances were opportunities to gain supernatural power. The dancers would try to become like blue jays, which they thought had sacred powers. They might use this power to cure or to predict the future.

Like other Peoples, the Kutenais had sweat lodge ceremonies. These are still held, and can be dangerous to those who are not properly trained because they can become dehydrated and hyperventilate. Inside the sweat lodge, men and women pray and try to purify themselves. Sometimes, they take breaks to swim in cold lakes or streams.

In the 1800s, Catholic priests thought it was important that they teach Native Americans about European ways to "enlighten" them. They insisted that the Native Americans stop all of their dancing and ceremonies. However, in general, the people responded by having even more frequent and extravagant ceremonies and potlatches.

## Festival to Honor Seals

At the end of the year in the Arctic, the Bering Sea Yupiks had a ceremony known as the Bladder Festival. They believed that every animal had a soul and should be treated with respect and reverence. When they hunted seals in spring and summer, they saved the animals' swim bladders because they believed that, when the animal died, its spirit went into its bladder. At the ceremony, they inflated the bladders and hung them up in the back of the kashim, or men's meeting house. Villagers sang, danced, and feasted, honoring the spirits of the seals. Finally, they brought the bladders to the ocean, deflated them, and sank them beneath the waves. They believed these spirits would be born again as new seals the following year.

# Timeline

## 1600s
The Anishinabe Medicine Society's Midewiwin Dance begins to be performed.

## 1750s
By now, almost every Plains Nation has a four-day Sun festival.

## 1816
Petalesharo sets the enemy girl free during the Pawnee Captive Girl Sacrifice, leading to the end of this ceremony.

## 1885
Canadian law made the potlatch illegal.

## 1890s
The Ghost Dance becomes popular among Plains Nations.

## 1910
The U.S. government outlaws the Sun Dance among Plains Native Americans because of its torturous elements.

## 1920s
Powwows gain popularity and begin to involve two or more Nations.

## 1970s
The National Eagle Repository is established to provide eagle feathers for Native American ceremonies and regalia.

## 1978
The American Indian Religious Freedom Act is passed. It protects the traditional religious rites and cultural practices of Native Americans and Alaska Natives.

## 1983
The first Gathering of Nations Powwow was held at University of Albuquerque in New Mexico.

## 1990
The Native American Graves Protection and Repatriation Act is passed, protecting Native American grave sites and demanding the return of bones and ceremonial artifacts to Native American Nations.

## 2018
Some 3,000 people perform in the annual Gathering of the Nations Powwow, which attracts about 72,000 spectators.

# Quiz

**1** In the Northwest, who was in charge of ceremonies?

**2** What were the four sacred rituals of the Midwinter Ceremony?

**3** When did the Cherokee Nation hold its Green Corn Ceremony?

**4** Why did Navajos hold the Blessing Way Ceremony?

**5** How did Achumawai girls celebrate puberty?

**6** Why was the Powamu Festival important for Hopi children?

**7** Which Nation started powwows, and what were they originally called?

**8** Which Nation held a Sacred Arrow Ceremony?

**9** Name three of the gifts that were commonly given at a potlatch.

**10** What was the Bladder Festival?

**Answers** **1.** A shaman **2.** Feather Dance, Thanksgiving Dance, Personal Chant, and Bowl Game **3.** When the last corn crop had ripened **4.** To bring good luck and protection **5.** With a 10-day feast **6.** Children of about 8 years old were initiated into kachina societies. **7.** The Poncas, and a powwow was originally called a hethuska. **8.** The Cheyenne **9.** Boxes, eulachon fish, chilkats, copper, carvings, songs **10.** It was a festival to honor the spirits of seals.

# Key Words

**conch:** a large, spiral shell from a marine snail

**condolence:** an expression of sympathy

**decompose:** slowly broken down through natural processes

**dehydration:** a dangerous reduction in the amount of water in the body

**exploited:** used unfairly for one's own advantage

**initiate:** a person who is being instructed in the customs of a group or organization

**kiva:** an underground room believed by Pueblos to be a doorway to the world of their ancestors

**lacrosse:** a team game in which players use a long-handled stick that has a mesh pouch at the end for catching, carrying, and throwing a ball at a goal

**mourning:** the expression of grief when someone has died

**potlatch:** an extravagant feast that includes abundant gift giving

**powwows:** Native American festivals that include feasting, singing, music, and dancing

**quilling:** craftwork that involves piercing something (usually fabric) with a hollowed-out feather

**recitations:** readings of something aloud, usually in public

**regalia:** special clothing, usually for a ceremony

**revered:** respected and honored

**ritual:** a formal ceremony that is always performed the same way

**shamans:** healers, or holy men or women

**status:** the rank or place of a person or family within their group

**supernatural:** something that cannot be explained by science and that seems to relate to another world

**tepee:** a cone-shaped shelter, usually covered with buffalo skin, that was used as a portable home by Plains Nations

**unique:** the only one of its kind

# Index

# LIGHTBOX

## SUPPLEMENTARY RESOURCES

Click on the plus icon ⊕ found in the bottom left corner of each spread to open additional teacher resources.

- Download and print the book's quizzes and activities
- Access curriculum correlations
- Explore additional web applications that enhance the Lightbox experience

## LIGHTBOX DIGITAL TITLES
### Packed full of integrated media

**VIDEOS**

**INTERACTIVE MAPS**

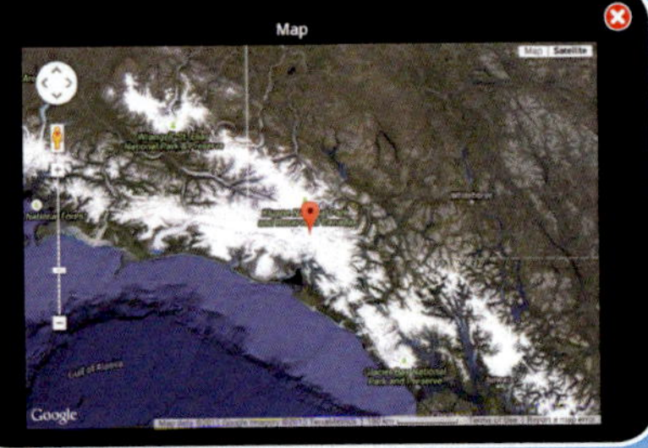


**WEBLINKS**

**SLIDESHOWS**

**QUIZZES**

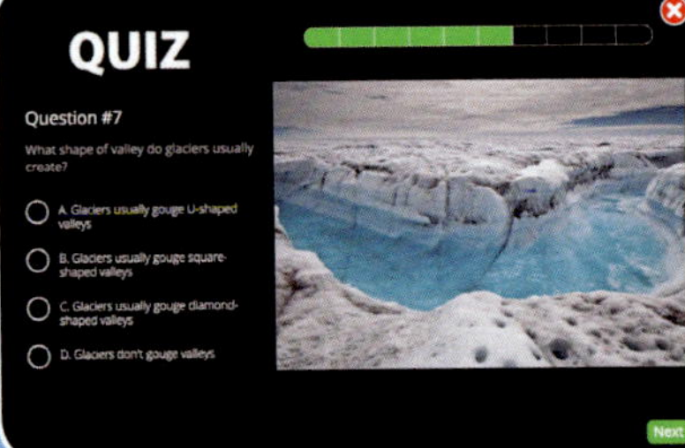


**OPTIMIZED FOR**
- ✓ TABLETS
- ✓ WHITEBOARDS
- ✓ COMPUTERS
- ✓ AND MUCH MORE!


Published by Smartbook Media Inc.
350 5th Avenue, 59th Floor New York, NY 10118
Website: www.openlightbox.com





First published by Mason Crest in 2014.

Library of Congress Control Number: 2018941491

ISBN 978-1-5105-3937-2 (hardcover)
ISBN 978-1-5105-3938-9 (multi-user eBook)

Printed in the Brainerd, Minnesota, United States
1 2 3 4 5 6 7 8 9 0 22 21 20 19 18

062018
121117

Project Coordinator: Heather Kissock
Designer: Ana María Vidal

Every reasonable effort has been made to trace ownership and to obtain permission to reprint copyright material. The publisher would be pleased to have any errors or omissions brought to its attention so that they may be corrected in subsequent printings.

The publisher acknowledges Alamy, Bridgeman Images, Getty Images, iStock, and Shutterstock as the primary image suppliers for this title.